Published by

Connected North

ISBN 978-0-578-70762-4

Twelve Months of Fun on Haida Gwaii with Mattie & Jojo

Story by Carsen Gray and Lynn Hughan

Illustrations by Lynn Hughan

As we experience changes in weather during the different times of year, this delightful book highlights adventures of two children learning together and connecting to the land. Aspects of Haida language and culture are woven throughout the story.

Organized by the months of the year, this book offers many teachable moments about the importance of our relationship with family, one another and the land that sustains us.

Over the past three years, TakingITGlobal's **Connected North** program has collaborated with **Sk'aadgaa Naay Elementary School in Skidegate, Haida Gwaii** as one of our community partners. I have very much enjoyed my visits to the community and the opportunities it offered to appreciate the beauty of Haida Gwaii. I have been impressed with meeting so many talented artists, including Carsen and Lynn, during my travels, and value the opportunity to collaborate on this special Haida story and resource.

We are grateful to the **Skidegate Haida Immersion Program (SHIP)**, a unique initiative that has provided edits and translations for the book and is doing important work to preserve and revitalize the Haida language.

We hope our work in co-developing resources like this one supports students in their own learning, strengthens community connections and further contributes to language revitalization efforts.

JENNIFER CORRIERO
Executive Director,
TakingITGlobal & Connected North

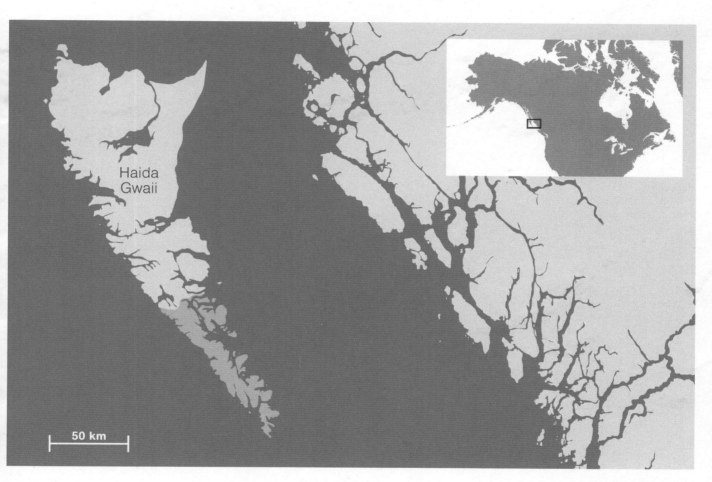

Haida
Gwaii

50 km

Courtesy of Hakai Magazine

This book is dedicated to

Nanaay,

(Gramma)

whose beach will always be an adventure,
and whose house is always a home.

Haida Gwaii

Mattie & Jojo live in Haida Gwaii.

Haida Gwaii is an island off the North Coast of British Columbia and is home to the Haida people. Mattie and his little sister Jojo love living here because there are so many fun things for children to see and do.

Every day is an adventure!

There is the **Tang.ᴳwan** *(ocean)*, **Chiix̱waay** *(beaches)*, **Hlk'inx̱adaay** *(forests)* with giant **Ts'uu** *(red cedar trees)*, and parks so everyday there are amazing things to do, every month brings something new!

Come along with Mattie and Jojo on a twelve-month journey!

What adventures does each month bring?

January
Taada K̲ung

(Cold Moon)

January is cold and **Taajuuwaay** *(windy)*. The cold north wind brings clear skies. and when it changes, the **T'aaGaaw K'amdawung** *(snow)* comes down. Mattie and Jojo climb into their snowsuits and head to the park in Skidegate. There is always time for fun in the snow. Daddy and Mommy have packed up snacks and a carrot to make the snowman a nose. The children roll the snow into balls and pile them one on the other. They find **Hlgaa skaats'ixulda** *(pebbles)* in the snow and use them for the snowman's eyes, smile and his buttons.

The carrot is placed carefully as the nose and Mattie and Jojo use sticks from the ground to make his arms.

He is a wonderful snowman!

February
Sg̱an T'aal Ḵung
(Flounder Moon)

February on Haida Gwaii can be chilly and, because the island is in the north, the sun sets in the sky by late afternoon. Mattie and Jojo go to school in the morning and play in the afternoon. They go out to play, but only on the sunny days.

February brings a **Yahguudang.nga** *(special)* day in the middle of the month.

Do you know what that special day is?

It's Valentine's Day! On Valentine's Day the kids make cards from paper and give them to friends and family that they **K'uuga** *(love)*.

March is a special month for Mattie and Jojo.

The weather is getting better, and the days are getting longer! March is also special because it is Mattie's birthday. Mattie receives some great gifts, but one present from his **Nanaay** is really special — a fancy kite! Mommy and Daddy take them to Jungle Beach where they could fly the **Gina náang xiidal** *(kite)*.

It is so much fun! Jojo runs on the beach chasing the kite while Mattie learns how to make the kite soar this way and that.

14

March
Ga Taa Gii Hal<u>x</u>a <u>K</u>ung
(Food Gathering Moon)

In **April** and throughout the year, Mattie and Jojo go to the **Hl<u>G</u>aagilda** Haida dance group. It is so much fun. The children learn the traditional songs and dances and get to see their friends. **S<u>K</u>áanaay** *(aunty)* Jenny is the instructor.

One special day the kids were able to go to Antler Cove where **S<u>K</u>áanaay** *(aunty)* Jenny lives to **Gaawjaaw** *(drum)* and sing with her. An **<u>G</u>uud** *(eagle)* watched from overhead. The eagle tilted his head and listened to the drum until he flew off over the trees singing his eagle song.

April
K'aawdang Ḵung
(Herring Roe on Kelp Moon)

May
Taa<u>x</u>id <u>K</u>ung
(Sockeye Moon)

It's **May**, spring time on Haida Gwaii, and the sun is shining more and more! The family goes on walks through the parks and beaches in Skidegate and Queen Charlotte, **Daajing Giids Llnagaay**.

Mattie loves swinging on the **Kaan.niiya** *(swings)* at the beach, while Jojo collects rocks near the water.

Nanaay has the best beach to play on in Skidegate.

In **June**, the children spend hours playing in the sand, searching for **Ts'aa.am skay** *(tiny crabs)* that live beneath the rocks. Mattie carefully lifts rocks to search for the hiding crabs. He enjoys watching them scurry off in all directions, searching for new rocks to hide under. Mattie catches the tiny ones and lets them walk in his hands before gently putting them back in the sand.

Jojo would rather **HlGay** *(dig)* with her **Gaasdluu.uu** *(shovel)* and bucket and watch the birds flying out over the water.

June
Sg̱aahlan K̲'al K̲ung
(Yellow Cedar Bark Moon)

July is warm and sunny. Mattie and Jojo love to play outside, and spend many days going to the **Chii<u>x</u>waay** *(beach)*.
They have many adventures!

The best is on the way!

The **S<u>G</u>aana** *(killer whales)* are travelling by. The orcas travel in groups called pods and they visit Haida Gwaii for many reasons throughout the year. The children are lucky on this day as they are close enough to hear them blowing water out of their blowholes and singing in the ocean.

22

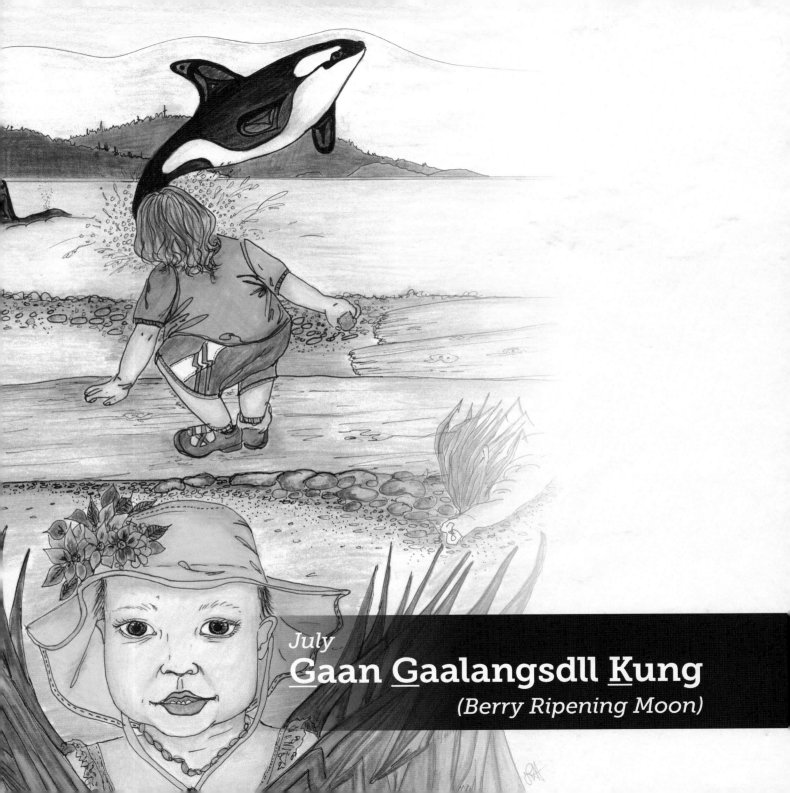

July
Gaan Gaalangsdll Kung
(Berry Ripening Moon)

August
Chiina K̲ung
(Salmon/Fish Moon)

In **August**, so many types of berries grow on Haida Gwaii. There are **SK'awGan** *(salmon berries)*, **SGiidllGuu** *(huckleberries)*, **Guugadiis** *(thimbleberries)* and Mattie and JoJo's favourite, **Gaan hlGahl** *(blackberries)*.

Can you guess who else loves berries?

Brother **Taan** *(black bear)* loves berries even more than the children! Bears need to eat as much as they can until the late fall so that they can pack on weight for the winter sleep.

25

Now it is **September**. Into the fall, the **St'all naay** *(chanterelles)* start to grow on the forest floor.

The sun and the rain help them grow. The kids enjoy searching for the yellow mushrooms hiding in the moss while a **X̲uuya** *(raven)* teases them from the spruce branches up above.

Raven flies from tree to tree hoping the kids will give him a treat.

September
Sk'aagii Ḵung
(Chum/Dog Salmon Moon)

October
'Waahlg̲ahl K̲ung
(Potlatch Moon)

On Haida Gwaii, **October** is filled with family gatherings and fun times. Thanksgiving in early October brings everyone together. All the little children get excited, wondering what costumes they will have for **K'aadxan Sii.ngaay** *(Halloween)*.

Every year, the family go to **Nanaay**'s house to carve **HlGuugaga** *(scary)* pumpkins, give out candy, and trick-or-treat.

There are so many children walking the streets of Skidegate all dressed up with their glow sticks and trick-or-treat bags. JoJo helps hand out treats while Daddy walks with Mattie until he gets so tired and has to be carried back home.

November
Taan Chaagan K'aadii Kung
(Black Bear Hibernate Moon)

By **November**, winter is coming again to Haida Gwaii. Mattie and Jojo are spending more time indoors. One of their favourite things to do is go to the library in Charlotte.

Story time with Patrick is a favourite! He likes to **Kuugin King dii** *(read)* books to the kids. The children all gather around for his felt stories, puppets and **SGaalang** *(songs)* he **K'aajuu** *(sings)* with the guitar!

What a wonderful way to have fun.

December is a busy time on Haida Gwaii. There are many craft fairs and so much to see and do. **Sah 'Laana K̲iiG̲aay Sii.ngaay** *(Christmas)* is in the air!

The children love going to the lighting of the Christmas tree at the Spirit Square, and Kay Christmas at the Haida Heritage Centre. There are so many fun activities: crafts and goodie bags, Christmas Cookies and more, but the best part of the fair is when **Sk̲'yuuG̲aay G̲aadas** *(Santa Claus)* arrives.

Mattie is happy to sit on Santa's lap with his wish list but little sister Jojo wants to see Mommy!

December
T'aagaaw Ḵung
(Snow Moon)

So **Hltaaxuulang** *(friends)*, as you can see these are just some of the fun and wonderful things that Mattie and Jojo enjoy in each of the twelve months of the year on Haida Gwaii!

Should you come to visit one day, these are some ideas for you and your family to try!

Twelve Months of Fun on Haida Gwaii with Mattie & Jojo

Story by Carsen Gray and Lynn Hughan

Illustrations by Lynn Hughan

To listen to the **audio book**,

visit *www.connectednorth.org/12monthsinhg*

Manufactured by Amazon.ca
Bolton, ON

29303718R00024